Spiritual Identity Theft Exposed

Doug Addison

www.DougAddison.com

Spiritual Identity Theft Exposed

ISBN-13: 978-0-9824618-1-5

ISBN-10: 0-9824618-1-X

Printed in USA by
InLight Connection
PO Box 7049
Santa Maria, CA 93456

Cover design: Cathy Arkle

For ordering information contact:

InLight Connection
(800) 507-7853

www.DougAddison.com

Table of Contents

Our Spiritual Identity..3

Strategy 1: We Believe That We Are Our Behavior...............................9

Strategy 2: Dying Too Much to Yourself and Losing Your Passion.... 13

Strategy 3: Get You to Believe You Are a Victim................................. 17

Strategy 4: Get You to Believe Your Negative Thoughts Are True..... 21

Strategy 5: Get You to Not Move Forward Because You are Afraid... 25

Strategy 6: Get Your Past Wounds to Rob Your Future 29

Strategy 7: Cause You to Not Forgive Others...................................... 33

Remedy 1: Develop a Positive Kingdom Perspective.......................... 37

Remedy 2: Seeing Ourselves as God Sees Us 41

Remedy 3: How to Change Instantly—The Power of Refocusing...... 45

Remedy 4: Realize that God Wants to Use Your Current Situation ... 49

Remedy 5: Develop the Lost Art of Revelation................................... 53

Remedy 6: Find Your Destiny 57

Remedy 7: God's Good Intentions for You 63

Doug Addison

Introduction

You don't have to look very far to find someone who has suffered from the effects of identity theft. I had a series of dreams in which God spoke to me about a plan from darkness that is trying to rob people of not only their credit cards and financial privacy, but also their destinies in God.

Oftentimes, things that are happening in the natural realm reflect or are symbolic of what is happening in the spiritual realm. You can see this principle throughout the Bible. An example is when Jesus was born; a new star appeared in the sky (Matthew 2:1–2). When He was crucified there was thick darkness in the afternoon and an earthquake happened that split the veil that separated the Holy of Holies in the temple of Jerusalem (Matthew 7:51–54).

The rise of identity theft in the world today is symbolic of what is happening spiritually to people all around the world. People are suffering from "spiritual identify theft." A plan from darkness has been released on the earth to blind people to their identity in God and from knowing their full potential of whom they could actually be. God has no limits and what we can do through His power and love has no limits as well. The only limits we have are self-imposed.

In 2004, while living in Los Angeles I was awakened in the middle of the night and a beautiful golden-skinned angel with long golden braids dressed in white was hovering over me whispering in my ear. I was given strategies from God on how to help people find and fulfill their destiny. I began to study and write about it and in the years since this encounter I have helped tens of thousands of people find and fulfill their destiny. In 2006 I was living in Moravian Falls, North Carolina, where I received more revelation and wrote my book, "Personal Development God's Way."

On Christmas morning of 2009 I woke to God speaking the words to me, "spiritual identity theft." This book contains the prophetic insight that God has been giving me about the covert strategies that Satan is trying to use against people to keep them from seeing, finding, and fulfilling their life purpose and destiny in God. It also has remedies and practical steps we can take that will radically turn around the direction of our lives. Some of it is from revelation I received through dreams, other parts from angelic visitations and some I developed while writing a book about life purpose and destiny in a cabin in Moravian Falls, North Carolina. I hope this short and to-the-point book will make its way to those who need it and that there will be a restoration of who we truly are in Christ.

Doug Addison

Santa Maria, California 2011

Our Spiritual Identity

Throughout the Bible we see God's plan for people unfold. In the Garden of Eden (Genesis 3) God was in direct relationship with Adam and Eve. He walked in the garden with them and allowed them to eat from the tree of life that was the source of their immortality. In this garden paradise there was also the tree of the knowledge of good and evil and God had told them not to eat the fruit of that tree or they would die (lose their immortality).

As the story goes, the serpent (Satan) got them to believe that if they ate the fruit of tree of the knowledge of good and evil their eyes would be opened and they would be like God, knowing good and evil. As they found out, Satan was lying to them and they were robbed of their true spiritual identity. The two trees in the garden represent the two sources of spirituality or spiritual identity. The tree of life is the spiritual source that is pure and from God and now awaits us in Heaven (Revelation 22). The second is the tree of the knowledge of good and evil.

God's original intention for us was to only know and experience pure life in a world that had no sickness or death. The fact that "God is love" (1 John 4:8) is an amazing revelation about His character and when bad things happen to us it is not from God. It is interesting to note that the tree of knowledge of good and evil has a mixture of good intentions, yet the possibility of evil results.

The good news is that we have been restored in our spiritual relationship with God through Jesus Christ. I am not going to preach to you in this book, but I do want to remind people that as I reveal these strategies of Satan to destroy us, God is much more powerful and desires to bring an amazing amount of acceptance, love, and unlimited power into our lives. You can have a close relationship with God as was originally intended. However, we will still battle with the fact that we also have the temptation and pull by Satan to live our life and use our gifts in a mixture of "good and evil."

The Good and Evil Mixture

Satan helped open the possibilities of "good and evil" into the world. We no longer have just pure life and love, but now we can have good intentions that can get tweaked or distorted. An example is that you can have wealth and use your money to help people in need. Then again, people with great wealth can be tempted with greed and power that will result in being unjust and ripping people off.

This good and evil mixture is a tension we all experience. We are all given gifts from God—some from birth. Some of these gifts lie dormant until we are spiritually awakened (or born again) and we invite the Holy Spirit into our life. We are all born with an amazing potential to fulfill the highest destiny and purpose in God, yet we drop down to what we think we can do. God's love and power have no limits and what we can accomplish with His Holy Spirit working through us has no limits either. Spiritual identity theft occurs when Satan tries to get you to think that you don't have these gifts and potential and that you have no clear destiny.

I have found after working with thousands of people through Life Coaching and my seminars that the areas of your life where you are experiencing the most attack or resistance may very well be an indicator of what some of your gifts and callings are. Why would Satan waste time attacking you if you did not have a great destiny to fulfill?

In my case, I had a recurring nightmare from an early age that I was being chased by something evil. I would be frozen in place and could not move in the dream. For years I would wake up running and screaming loudly through my house. This was alarming to my family and later my roommates. They thought I had psychological problems but what they did not realize was there is a destiny I have in God that Satan did not want me to fulfill. I now help people who are stuck and not able to move forward in their lives. I also have discovered that there are many dreams that we can have at night that point toward our life dreams.[1] After I began pursuing my destiny in this area the nightmares went away. God had given me this gift early on in my life and He intended me to use it for good. But Satan caused it to be mixed with evil to try to stop me from seeing it.

There is a viewpoint held by some Christians that if we can avoid sin at all costs and become holy, then we will have a close relationship with God. Though there is truth in this, it has its downside. We can become so focused on avoiding sin that it becomes all we think about. Then Satan comes along and brings the mixture of evil to our good efforts. If we are spending a lot of effort on being holy then

---

[1] See Personal Development God's Way by Doug Addison, Chapter 10.

there is a chance that we feel guilty and condemned when we have areas of our life that have not been worked out yet. The Holy Spirit will convict us of our sin but Satan tries to condemn us, causing us to feel separated from God when we sin.

A better approach to holiness is getting into a close relationship with God by placing our focus on His goodness and love for us. Yes, repent when you fall short, but if you put your energy toward doing good and loving others instead of avoiding sin you will find yourself sinning less. This too is a strategy of Satan to steal away our most basic and profound identity that we are sons and daughters of God and can have a relationship with Him that is not based on rules but on the Father's great love and the Son's great sacrifice for us.

I am going to reveal several strategies that Satan will attempt to use against us and I'll provide several remedies as well. This is not intended to inflict fear or to get you to focus too much on the attacks of Satan. It is simply meant to bring these plans into the light so you can put a plan of action in place and go for all that God has for you in your life.

Missing Your Destiny

Here is a good example of someone missing their destiny in the Bible. In Luke 18:18–25, Jesus was nearing the end of His ministry on earth with only a few weeks left before He was to fulfill His destiny by dying on the cross. A rich young leader asked Him what he should do to inherit eternal life. Jesus answered him with the steps he needed to take and then went on to tell him that he lacked one thing: he needed to give his money to the poor and follow Him.

It is interesting that Jesus uses the same words, *"follow me,"* that He did when He called Peter, James, and John to be disciples (Matthew 4:19). The young man went away discouraged because it would have cost him all his wealth. Some people think that Jesus was telling us that we should not have wealth. I see it from a different angle. I think that this rich young man would most likely have been the replacement for Judas, who handled the finances for Jesus' ministry. Judas was the one who betrayed Jesus and later hanged himself. Jesus may very well have been trying to "headhunt" a successor for Judas as one of the twelve disciples.

Since the young leader had not been following Jesus for three years like the rest, Jesus may have been trying to fast-track him into being a disciple. This would have required the man to get through the things that had held him back. In his case, it was the love of money. The rich young man missed his destiny in God. He was afraid of losing his earthly possessions. As he walked away, Jesus made a promise:

"I tell you the truth," Jesus said to them, "no one who has left home or wife or brothers or parents or children for the sake of the kingdom of God will fail to receive many times as much in this age and, in the age to come, eternal life." (Luke 18:29–30)

This young man may have suffered from Spiritual Identity Theft. He told Jesus that he had obeyed all the laws and felt that he was doing what was right. He knew there was a higher purpose in his life. Satan used a strategy of greed to hold him back from a greater destiny. With God there is always another chance! Many people never reach true fulfillment in life because they fall into some of the strategies I am going to reveal in this book. Again, as I begin to reveal the plans that Satan has against us, it is not meant to instill fear or to cause you to focus on negative things in your life. As you will find in this book, I will talk a lot about the ability to turn our focus away from negative things and toward God and his positive love and power to change our lives. I will also reveal some remedies that will help you to overcome the plans of the enemy and get you into a bright new future.

Strategy 1: We Believe That We Are Our Behavior

Bad experiences or painful life situations from our past can negatively affect our present life. There are forces of darkness that want us to believe that we are the only ones who suffer with these issues and that they are unchangeable. This is simply not true. Too often our sin and emotional baggage gets linked to what we believe about ourselves. In other words, our personality and identity become associated with the things we struggle with, as opposed to how God views us. This strategy of the enemy is for us to believe that we actually "are" how we feel or behave, which is far from reality.

Satan wants you to believe things like: you "are" depressed, unhappy, worthless, unable to change, stupid, a failure … the list could go on and on. It is important to realize that our feelings and behavior are situational and that we can change them—the reality is that feelings and behavior are not who we really are. These might be things that we struggle with, but they are not our identity, or who we are in Christ.

This includes the things that you may think about yourself at a deep level. You might not consciously believe them, but you find yourself thinking them or saying them about yourself on a regular basis. Most people don't see that there is a direct connection between the way they view themselves and their destiny.

"For as he thinks in his heart, so is he." (Proverbs 23:7a, NKJV)

Some of the things that we struggle and battle with in our daily lives usually come from a root cause, something

9

we have done, knowingly or unknowingly, or things that were done to us. Healing these emotional wounds can sometimes be a process. If you commit yourself to the journey you can overcome them. A key to recovery is to not beat yourself up each day. Instead, consider inviting God into your imperfection. He is not surprised by your behavior and God loves you just the same. Learn to enjoy your life even though you are not yet perfected.

My life turned around for the good when I realized one day that I spent too much time beating myself up for having negative or lustful thoughts. I remember the day that I invited God into my day to walk with me like a loving father would. I prayed and asked for an extra measure of grace to get me through each day. Surprisingly, when I stopped focusing on the negative thoughts and talked to God about them as they were happening, they began to lose their power over me and eventually became less of a driving force in my thought life.

We live in a therapeutic society that has a diagnosis for just about everything. When we start worrying about our dog suffering from Separation Anxiety Disorder, you know there is an over-focus on labeling people and situations in our lives. There is value in recognizing negative patterns in our lives and I am not trying to downplay the effects of pain, addiction and abuse. We need to find a way to identify it, get healed and move on from the recovery room so that our identity is in the new life God has given us, not the old life that tried to destroy us.

Too many people are content with living in a spiritual hospital and may not realize that you can be free. Just so you know, I suffered lots of pain in my past including physical, emotional and sexual abuse as a child. I spent half my life depressed until I realized that I could not live my life looking backwards. I will share with you later in this book how I was able to get free from the pain of my past.

Doug Addison

Strategy 2: Dying Too Much to Yourself and Losing Your Passion

Satan wants to steal our identities and take away any hope for change. When he is able to get us to believe the lies about ourselves in Strategy One, he then uses Bible verses out of context as he tried to do with Jesus (Matthew 4:1–11) to release a second deadly attack against our destinies by getting us to overreact to our sin. Satan came to Jesus to tempt him and used the Torah (Old Testament) to try to get Jesus to kill Himself but Jesus recognized the attack. This would have cut off the destiny of Jesus. Satan is still using this strategy with people today.

To experience a radically transformed life we must have renewed thinking. It is interesting that while writing about how to find God's will for your life, the Apostle Paul says that we must first change our thinking by renewing our minds.

"And do not be conformed to this world, but be transformed by the renewing of your mind, that you may prove what is that good and acceptable and perfect will of God."(Romans 12:2)

The process of renewing your mind involves a principle called dying to yourself. There are several verses in the Bible that talk about dying to the sinful nature or "old self" and allowing God to live through us. This is a necessary process for transforming your life. However, it is also a very misunderstood principle.

13

Satan wants to get us to take this to the extreme and believe that we must die to all the heart desires and plans that we have. In reality, dying to ourselves does not mean that we cannot have any desires or ideas of our own. If that were the case, you would become a robot for God. God wants us to be his sons and daughters and to have authority on the earth.

God created the Heavens and the earth and we are created in His image (Genesis 1:27). Therefore, we all have the ability to be co-creators to expand His Kingdom on earth. Whether you realize this or not, we are all creative and have a God-given ability and passion inside to create things around us. We have a built-in desire to contribute to things greater than ourselves and be a part of changing the world around us through God's unlimited love and power.

I often jokingly say that God was trying to prophesy this through Bruce Willis in the movie "Die Harder." God wants to give us good things and once our motives are right He can do this without limit. It is no wonder that so many people don't know their destiny; it may be because they have died to any desire they may have once had.

"Delight yourself in the LORD and he will give you the desires of your heart." (Psalms 37:4)

Dying to yourself means that your heart has the right intentions. Not all of our desires are necessarily from God. I remember when I was young I learned how to spell the word Christian. A lady told me it is spelled "Christ" plus the acronym i-a-n which stands for "I am nothing." I grew up believing that I was not allowed to be anything. I realize now that God wants us to be His creation. It will require

14

dying to our sinful desires but also living a life full of His creativeness.

Quite often God will give us a passion or strong desire to fulfill something in our lives. Passion is important because it brings about a divinely inspired drive to accomplish things for God. We do need a balance in all this. For example on one hand we don't want to be too prideful, and on the other we don't want false humility.

We often quote the Bible verse, *"He must become greater and I must become less..."* (John 3:30). The problem with false humility is when you try to become less without allowing God's character and gifts in you to become greater, you will be empty.

Doug Addison

Strategy 3: Get You to Believe You Are a Victim

This Strategy goes hand-in-hand with Strategies one and two. Satan does a "smoke and mirrors" behind-the-scenes maneuver to try and keep us from seeing the root causes that are holding us back from our destiny in God. There is a plan from darkness to get you to believe that all the bad things that may have happened to you in the past are the very reason you cannot succeed today.

I am not trying to invalidate the fact that you may have had a painful past. I actually have suffered more abuse and bad circumstances than the average person, and I had to get healed of the emotional effects that were left. I meet people all the time that protect their pain and past experiences and reject attempts to help them get through it.

This is a plan of the enemy to get us into a victim mentality where we blame others, even God, for why we are not able to move forward. This happened with Adam and Eve in Genesis Chapter 3 when they first lost their Spiritual Identity. Adam blamed Eve instead of owning up to the fact that he participated in the process.

We don't even have to have a painful past to suffer from this strategy, which will, if not dealt with, derail your future. Most of us were raised in a blame-shifting environment. We may not recognize it because it is so common. The first step to changing ourselves is to recognize that there is a problem with grumbling and making excuses. Excuses are disempowering, especially when we start believing them.

Here are a few examples of blame-shifting. People might say that they are not able to save any money because they have too many bills to pay which places the blame on the bills as opposed to their financial responsibility. However, the reality is that they could spend less or make more.

When someone tells me that they can't get ahead financially because they pay too much in rent and taxes, I suggest that they move to a cheaper place and consult with a tax expert to make sure they aren't paying too much in taxes. You can make more money or spend less. You are not a victim to your financial situation.

How about when people say they don't have enough time to exercise. I wonder how much television they watch. You can always do a few exercises in front of the tube. Time is one thing we all have in common. Finding ways to use it effectively is usually the real issue.

When we take responsibility for our actions and situations, we gain back control. We always have choices. If you are not able to change a situation, then you can at least change the way you respond to it. You have a choice!

Victims give up their power and right to make decisions for themselves and think they are stuck with what happened to them. The good news is that you do have the power to change and oftentimes, it is as easy as changing the way you view your life and current situation.

When I grew up I got a Ph.D. in excuses! Since then I have learned that you cannot change the past, but you can change the way it affects you in the present. And when you begin to change your present situation in any way, then you are ultimately changing your future.

The fastest way to do this is to start taking 100% responsibility for everything you do. When we use excuses, we are being victims. Victims believe that they have no control over what happens to them. They allow themselves to be controlled by the things that happen around them.

A victim mentality blinds you to your own faults, causes you to think everyone is out to get you, blames the current situation, or pins your problems on others because of their decisions or actions, and keeps you in a continual spinning cycle that has no end. It can cause you to be addicted to the attention you get when you share your latest drama. We will never be able to stop "stuff" that happens to us, but we can change the way we respond to it.

Doug Addison

Strategy 4: Get You to Believe Your Negative Thoughts Are True

We all have a story or something that has happened to shape us, whether positive or negative. This strategy goes hand-in-hand with a victim mentality. Bad things happen to us and we have to be careful that we do not let all our past hurts, failures, and negative experiences derail us from our future.

Our story can become like a breaker switch, automatically shutting us down and hindering us when we get under pressure. This can happen when we begin to grow and succeed as well. Ever notice that when things start to go well for you then suddenly you start being drawn to old behaviors and thoughts? Most of the time it happens at a subconscious level and we are not aware of it. As this strategy of the enemy is revealed then you will most certainly be aware of it in your life.

When things start to go well or your life starts to heat up it is possible that you begin to feel uncomfortable and, like a breaker switch, you begin to shut things down by distracting yourself with overworking or checking out in some way. Left unchecked, your past experiences can negatively affect your future.

Here are some symptoms that the past is still affecting you:

- You have feelings of revenge or can't get a past hurt out of your mind

- You find yourself avoiding things you know you need to do
- You tried once or twice and have not tried since
- You are afraid of making mistakes or being rejected
- You avoid trying new things

"Therefore, if anyone is in Christ, he is a new creation; the old has gone, the new has come!" (2 Corinthians 5:17)

Maturing in your spiritual life is not an instant thing. As a matter of a fact, it is a lifelong process. Invite God into your imperfection—too often we allow feelings of failure to separate us from the life and love of God. Your current life situation is a direct result of what you believe and do on a regular basis. Our story from the past can negatively affect our internal thinking, which consists of thoughts and beliefs that are often contrary to God's Word and His ways.

Past experiences or negative things spoken to us, particularly when we were young, can get embedded in our minds. We begin to believe these things even though they are not true. Phrases like, "you're stupid; you'll never make anything of yourself; you will not succeed; you don't deserve this …" are ungodly, disempowering beliefs.

For the longest time, I seriously believed that I was not very smart. It held me back from going to college and stepping out in my gifts and talents.

"Therefore, prepare your minds for action; be self-controlled; set your hope fully on the grace to be given you when Jesus Christ is revealed." (1 Peter 1:13).

Consider the fact that when you focus on the negative parts of your life you are constantly dealing with negative things. Continual focus on what you cannot do or what you are struggling with will cause the negative thinking to persist. Instead, redirect your thoughts to something good, like Peter said, "Think about the grace that will be given to you."

"Finally, brothers, whatever is true, whatever is noble, whatever is right, whatever is pure, whatever is lovely, whatever is admirable—if anything is excellent or praiseworthy—think about such things." (Philippians 4:8)

Paul also talks about developing the fruit (or evidence) of the Spirit in us: love, joy, peace, patience, kindness, goodness, faithfulness, gentleness, and self-control (Galatians 5:22–23). Peter wrote about how to develop a divine nature.

"For this very reason, make every effort to add to your faith goodness; and to goodness, knowledge; and to knowledge, self-control; and to self-control, perseverance; and to perseverance, godliness; and to godliness, brotherly kindness; and to brotherly kindness, love." (2 Peter 1:5–7)

A story from the past and negative internal thinking can be easily turned around by thinking the opposite or positive thoughts about yourself. It sounds too good to be true but it is the starting place. When I first started writing and speaking about this concept, people told me that it is not that easy.

Renewing your mind from the negative thoughts that have been programmed in you will take time. I recommend making a list of the negative things that you think to yourself. Things like, "I'm ugly, I'm stupid, I will never make it …" Write the opposite next to each one. Begin telling yourself that you are God's beautiful creation and that you have the mind of Christ. When the negative thought comes, turn it around and eventually you will be thinking the positive.

Strategy 5: Get You to Not Move Forward Because You are Afraid

Why are most people not pressing in to all that God has for them? A major reason is fear. A strategy of Satan is to get you to hold back because of fear. This could be fear of failure, fear of succeeding, fear of rejection, fear of man, fear of … you fill in the blanks.

I meet people all the time who are afraid to make decisions because they fear that they will be wrong or that it will be outside of God's timing. This causes them to stay in a neutral position in life. This is exactly where Satan wants you to stay. You might have a good intention of making the right choices, but not making decisions is not the solution. The fact is that we all learn by mistakes and God does not mind you making a few if your intent is not evil.

We all have some type of fear in our lives and the funny part is that the fear is not usually based in reality. You can recognize when you or someone you know has fear just by the way you talk and view life. If you find yourself using words like, "I'm afraid, I would be scared, that terrifies me …" then you probably have a good amount of fear that is most likely holding you back in some area of your life.

The words "do not be afraid" appear in the Bible nearly 70 times. That's a lot.

But now, this is what the Lord says— … "Fear not, for I have redeemed you; I have summoned you by name; you are mine. When you pass through the waters, I will be with you; and when you pass through the rivers, they will not sweep over you. When you walk through the fire, you will not be burned; the flames will not set you ablaze." (Isaiah 43:1–2)

The best way to deal with fear is to recognize it for what it is and move forward. The Bible tells us that fear is not just an emotion but it can be a spirit as well.

"For God has not given us a spirit of fear, but of power and of love and of a sound mind." (2 Timothy 1:7 NKJV)

Sometimes we don't move forward into our destiny, or we are not able to change because we don't know what we want. But when you know what you want and yet you are not able to break through or follow through, then what's really stopping you may be fear. A major key to overcoming fear is to simply recognize it and storm right through it. Fear is like jet engines that can propel you in the opposite direction of your destiny. But if you just turn them around they can propel you in the correct direction or right into your life's purpose. Do something practical to overcome your fear like take a class, read a book, or do some research.

I meet a lot of people who are afraid of being deceived by some false teaching or doctrine. It is good to be cautious but if we are operating in fear we might reject something new that God is trying to teach us. A good way to avoid being deceived is to get to know God's ways and character and practice hearing his voice on a regular basis.

"But solid food is for the mature, who by constant use have trained themselves to distinguish good from evil." (Hebrews 5:14)

If you use your gifts consistently then you will recognize what is true and what is false. This will break the strategy of fear that Satan tries to inflict to keep us from moving forward.

I used be afraid to read aloud and speak in public. Now this is what I do for a living and I love it. I am still not where I'd like to be as far as reading aloud, but I have found ways to work through it. I started small and worked my way up. I led a small Bible study and volunteered to lead a junior high Sunday school group. There was a lot of grace with the kids and I found that if you can keep the attention of teenagers, you can do about anything in your life. I eventually asked if I could give a talk at a Sunday night service. I did the same at work. I led a small training and then asked to speak at the annual sales meeting on how to get orders processed faster.

Whatever we focus on continually can become our reality, whether it is rational or not. If we focus on why we cannot do something, we will never be able to do it. You might be focusing too much on how hard it is to change, instead of focusing on how easy it is to take small steps each day.

Doug Addison

Strategy 6: Get Your Past Wounds to Rob Your Future

A major strategy that Satan uses to steal our identity is to get us to focus on our past wounds and in turn allow them to rob us of a bright future. If you focus too much on the past you will lose your vision and begin to believe that you do not have a future.

Twenty years ago I began getting lots of deep healing in my life and growing in maturity towards my destiny. As I was reading the Bible one day, God drew my attention to the story of the resurrection of Christ.

Jesus was crucified and was buried and Mary Magdalene went to his tomb on Sunday morning. The stone in front of the tomb was rolled aside. She knelt down and looked inside, but His body was not there. He had been resurrected from the dead, but she didn't know where he was. She was crying because of her great loss. Here's the actual account from the Gospel of John.

Then the disciples went back to their homes, but Mary stood outside the tomb crying. As she wept, she bent over to look into the tomb and saw two angels in white, seated where Jesus' body had been, one at the head and the other at the foot. They asked her, "Woman, why are you crying?" "They have taken my Lord away," she said, "and I don't know where they have put him." At this, she turned around and saw Jesus standing there, but she did not realize that it was Jesus. "Woman," he said, "why are you crying? Who is it you are looking for?" Thinking he was the gardener, she said, "Sir, if you have carried him away, tell me where you have put him, and I will get him." Jesus said to her,

"Mary." She turned toward him and cried out in Aramaic, "Rabboni!" (which means Teacher). (John 20:10–16, NIV)

As I read this, my eyes were opened to a key for getting over painful events from the past. Mary was traumatized by witnessing the brutal beating and death of her friend, teacher, and Lord. Her pain was due to the traumatic loss of someone, who may have been the first to ever care for her.

Notice these key elements:

The Tomb: The other disciples had spent time mourning at the tomb of Jesus and then went back home, but Mary stayed there crying. Mary looked into the tomb and was focused on her loss.

This is similar to when we focus on the loss and pain of our past. Too often we can stay continually focused on the tomb of our past. There is no life in the tomb. Don't get me wrong, it is important to take time to deal with grief and loss, and yet there comes a time to look in a new direction. You cannot live your life in front of the tomb of your past perpetually. Get help to move through it. People everywhere are hanging around the tombs of their past losses.

Jesus was behind her: Notice where Jesus was as Mary stood crying looking into the tomb. He was standing behind her. Mary had to get up and turn 180 degrees away from the tomb. This symbolizes the need for us to turn our focus away from our past, and from our pain and loss. There is a time to grieve, but if you keep your focus on your loss, you will not recover from it.

The Gardener: As Jesus stood behind Mary he was actually mistaken for a gardener, that is, someone who helps cultivate new life. This symbolizes that when you turn your focus away from your loss, God is there to help things grow and bring life.

Meanwhile, back at the tomb, Mary saw two angels inside the tomb who were able to give her new direction. They represent the idea that inside every painful experience there is a blessing from God, if we can only recognize it.

When Jesus said, "Mary," her eyes were opened, and she immediately recognized him. Often, we are not able to recognize the work of God in our painful situation. God will do something to let us know that He knows where we are hurting and stuck.

In Mary's case, when He spoke her name, she then recognized Jesus. As you get in a close relationship with Him, God will find ways to let you know He loves and cares for you specifically. He will speak to you in some way that will let you know He knows you.

After reading this, I began to recognize that in every painful experience there was a gift and opportunity for us to grow. By simply changing your focus, you can allow the past to strengthen you and give you the necessary tools to help others who are camped out at their tombs.

The way to break this strategy of Satan and a key to a brighter future is the power of refocusing away from the past and onto God. Once you get a new perspective, the painful times can help strengthen you to fulfill your destiny in ways you could never have imagined.

Strategy 7: Cause You to Not Forgive Others

Another major strategy of Satan that will steal your identity and destiny is to get you to a place where you are not able to forgive other people when they have done something to hurt you. Forgiveness is a key to being able to live a spiritual life full of God's love and power.

I read an article called, "Forgiveness: A Key to Better Health." The following quotation says it all:

"Don't just talk about forgiveness. Researchers are finding that really forgiving others has important effects on your health. Forgiveness has long laid the foundation for spiritual well-being in the Judeo-Christian tradition. But scientific research now suggests its healing power may extend beyond the sacred realm. Research shows links between forgiveness and physical and mental health."

While this may come as some surprise to secular scientists, in the article psychologist Dan Shoultz says, "God has created the need to give and receive as an important part of our makeup as human beings. We were designed by God to not hold onto anger, revenge, bitterness, and resentment … When we do, it's destructive to our being, leading to a slow and insidious breakdown of the entire system."[2]

Many people suffering from stress, anxiety, bitterness, and depression may very well need to forgive themselves and others. The effects of bitterness and

---

[2] Vibrant Magazine, January 2001, Forgiveness: a Key to Better Health by Allison Kitchen

unforgiveness are not only physical but also spiritual. The Bible links forgiving others with being forgiven by God:

"For if you forgive men when they sin against you, your heavenly Father will also forgive you." (Matthew 6:14)

"Be kind and compassionate to one another, forgiving each other, just as in Christ God forgave you." (Ephesians 4:32)

If you have unforgiveness you may find yourself:

- Thinking about getting revenge
- Wanting something bad to happen to a person
- Holding a grudge
- Talking about someone behind their back
- Obsessing with a memory of something someone did to you

Forgiving a person does not mean that you agree with what they did.

- You can forgive a person, but trust may need to be rebuilt for the relationship to be restored.
- You can also forgive a person who is no longer living.
- You can forgive someone without telling him or her that you forgave them.
- It is the act of forgiveness that frees things up in the spiritual realm.
- Forgiving yourself is necessary as well. Just as unforgiveness can create negative effects—forgiving creates a positive atmosphere.

Steps to Forgiveness

List out the offenses that people have done that continue to bother you. You may have already forgiven them, but if you are still feeling the ill effects, then repeat the exercise.

Go through them one by one and ask God to give you the strength to forgive them. Say, "In the name of Jesus, I forgive _____ for _____."

Visually see yourself releasing the person. See the hurt you have been carrying vanish into God's light or the Cross of Christ. If you need to, write a letter to the person or to God. You don't have to mail it. This can be expressed to a person no longer living or to someone still alive. Be honest and feel the effects this pain has had on you, not the pain itself. The goal is to let it be released from you so it no longer affects you.

Decide if you want to talk with the person or not, but realize that confrontation may bring up the same response as you had before. Only do this if it is safe. It is not necessary to talk to a person to forgive them. Realize that forgiveness and healing is a process. It may take time. You may need to repeat this a few times.

It is not usually necessary to get up in front of your friends or church and confess publicly. You can forgive people in your heart and spirit and benefit from the process. As we get out of this strategy of not forgiving others we will most definitely see the benefits. It will have a positive effect on your mind and your body.

Remedy 1: Develop a Positive Kingdom Perspective

We have identified seven strategies that Satan can use against us that will result in Spiritual Identity Theft. As I mentioned previously, it is not my intent to get you to be fearful or put too much focus of the plans of the enemy. If you recognize any of these in your life simply pray and ask God to give you the strength and a remedy to overcome it. I have already given you some steps you can take, but now I want to give you strategies from God that you can implement into your life that will help build a solid spiritual foundation.

When we continually focus our attention on things that are wrong, negative, or that don't work, then we can start to see the world through a negative viewpoint and start believing this is the reality everywhere. Just watch the news on television and you can start thinking that things are very bad everywhere. Fear and hopelessness can set in, and we start thinking that the world is going down—so what is the use anyway? Well, the true reality is that God is still in charge and last I checked He is still in a good mood. His love and changing power are still available to us all. We must develop what Jesus referred to as "eyes that see." We must have the belief that nothing is too difficult for God.

God's love and power are much stronger than any demonic power. We have nothing to fear. It helps to get the perspective that powers of darkness in this world are trying to destroy God's creation. We must be careful not to buy into the lie that we are all doomed. So when we see someone suffering from things like depression, suicidal thoughts, or sickness, we must realize that this is not the will of God for this person or even ourselves. It is the plan of the enemy to steal their life and destiny. Because God's love and will for us are the only true reality, we must recognize the works of darkness as a counterfeit and deterrent to God's intentions for us.

We can learn a very powerful strategy in the encounters I just mentioned where Jesus encourages people to change their lives. The example of Mary peering into the tomb of Jesus, crying while Jesus was behind her calling her do a 180 degree turn away from her pain. Satan wanted Mary to focus on her pain and loss but Jesus was calling her to focus on the new life that He brings. When you see the works of darkness in a person's life, or your own for that matter, you have the opportunity to positively turn it around and bring God's love and encouragement which will lead to a new life.

"… The reason the Son of God appeared was to destroy the devil's work." (1 John 3:8)

I am always looking to encourage people who are suffering from negative influences. When I offer love and encouragement to others, I see the greatest changes happen in their lives. I have developed a strategy that I call "Fliptastic," or "flipping" a negative situation using a positive Kingdom perspective. It is the ability to recognize the negative things of Satan, turn them around and interject God's love and kindness into that situation. Suddenly, a light comes on where there was no hope. I see "mini-miracles" all the time by simply finding something positive in a person and pointing it out to them.

First John 4:4 tells us that the Spirit within us is greater than the one in the world around us (my paraphrase). Science has discovered that there is a major difference between light and dark. Light can be measured; it has substance and mass, and when it moves it has force. Darkness, however, is the absence of light. Jesus is Light, and Paul encourages us to live as children of Light. When we do this, we bring God's presence with us everywhere we go, even if we are not aware of it. Living our lives with a greater measure of God's love and light is extremely powerful. We dispel darkness, sometimes without having to say a word, because the Spirit within us is powerful and healing.

"For you were once darkness, but now you are light in the Lord. Live as children of light." (Ephesians 5:8)

We all need to understand and regularly practice the positive spiritual principles of praying for those who curse us, loving those who hate us, giving to those in need, helping the oppressed, being humble as opposed to proud and arrogant, forgiving those who offend us ... the list is actually too long to fully mention here, but you get the picture. Notice that most of these principles are relationally oriented. They teach us how to relate with others and with God.

We can change the spiritual atmosphere around us by loving, blessing, and being an encouragement everywhere we go. Many people love God, but when no one is looking, they can be guilty of mistreating or being mean to people. The fun part of focusing on blessing people is that, if you do these things regularly, the principle of sowing and reaping will eventually kick in. Your life will be overflowing with good things that you gave out to others, to the point that you cannot help but change the world around you. What you sow is what you will reap. If you sow grumbling, doubt, fear, depression, anxiety, and complaining, then that is what you will get in return.

Developing a positive Kingdom perspective and lifestyle is what will truly change our lives and the lives of many around us.

My wife and I encountered a businessman who had an obvious problem with alcohol and lust. He was divorced and had health problems, but after listening to him talk, I was able to pick up on the fact that he enjoyed giving to good causes. In spite of the man's negative persona, we were able to encourage him that his desire to give to others was a good trait and a gift that God had given him. It was a small start to help him realize that he has a greater purpose and that God cares for him.

Remedy 2: Seeing Ourselves as God Sees Us

The amazing thing about God is that when He sees your life He has a perspective that is way beyond ours. He somehow simultaneously looks at our past, sees our present struggles and knows our full potential in the future and … He loves us right where we are today. He deals with us according to the level of maturity that we are at right now and He does not require more than we can handle.

Most of the strategies of Satan deal with the fact that we all sometimes let the past hold us back from the future. This is because we have not learned to develop the ability of seeing ourselves as God sees us. If you want to stop allowing negative things from your past to control your present and future, it will involve changing old thought patterns.

"Do not conform any longer to the pattern of this world, but be transformed by the renewing of your mind. Then you will be able to test and approve what God's will is—his good, pleasing and perfect will," (Romans 12:2)

Renewing your mind involves replacing the old mindset with a new one. Your new mindset is who you are becoming, not who you have been. The good news is that this is the way that God sees you. When you come into line with God's intentions, you actually tap into His unlimited power to transform your life.

Here's how it works. God's purpose for you is to prosper you, give you hope and a future, and not harm you (Jeremiah 29:11). If you try to make changes in your life by focusing on what you should not do, then you are trying to live by rules and not by a relationship with God. God is relationship-oriented—that is why He refers to Himself as Father and to Jesus as His Son; this indicates that He wants to relate to us as family.

The Bible compares this transformation to stepping away from the picture of your old self and putting on a picture of your new self. God's focus is on you becoming who you were created to be. He relates to you according to this image. It is very important that you see yourself in this way as well.

One of the Apostle Paul's prayers for those he was training was that the eyes of their heart would be enlightened and that they would know the hope of their calling (see Eph. 1:18). The Greek word used for "know" is to "see or perceive." This goes deeper than just head-knowledge. When you see and perceive the hope of your calling, it causes you to take action because it is much more tangible and real.

God sees us as we are becoming or in other words, in our full potential. Here are some biblical examples illustrating this concept.

Judges 6: Gideon is hiding in fear, and an angel comes and calls him a mighty man of valor—God treated him according to the way He saw him in the future.

John 1:40–42: Simon had just met Jesus, he (Simon) is still flaky—Jesus tells him "You shall be called Cephas (or Peter, which means 'rock')." Jesus treated him the way He saw him in the future, not how he was at that moment.

Acts 9: Saul was murdering Christians, and then God knocked him to the ground on the road to Damascus. Before Saul's life was changed, God told Ananias to tell Saul that he is a chosen instrument and is a brother.

A real life example is someone like Nancy who never saw herself as a leader, let alone a business owner. She was a stay-at-home mom. When her son went off to college, she was challenged with finding the greater purpose for her life. She began getting clues about her destiny by asking others. One day she was able to get a glimpse that her potential in God had no limits. She began pursuing a dream of owning a corner store in her hometown. She got a business plan, and an SBA loan that took over two years. In the process she worked as a manager of a coffee shop to gain experience. She was able to start seeing herself as a leader, even though she had not led anything since high school.

The key is to begin to see yourself in your full potential in God. See yourself as God sees you, not as you once were, or even as you are now, but by faith getting a picture of who you are becoming in God. You might not be there yet, but if you begin seeing yourself there, then you will start changing your behavior to act differently. You will start coming into agreement with God for your life calling.

Remedy 3: How to Change Instantly—The Power of Refocusing

You can change your behavior right now, instantly, when you understand that you can refocus your thoughts or emotional energy away from the negative. This is because whatever you focus on becomes your reality.

"For as he thinks in his heart, so is he..." (Prov. 23:7, NKJV)

Let's say you are focusing on feeling bad about being in debt—most likely you will carry this negative baggage with you throughout your entire life. It is like a weight tied around your neck and shoulders. Instead, decide right now that you will put a debt reduction plan in place and get on with life.

Begin to refocus on finding creative ways to earn additional money and have fun in the process. Remember the spiritual principles of *"whatever you sow you will reap"* (Galatians 6:7) and *"If you believe you will receive"* (Matthew 21:22). In other words, where you focus your energy, you are making this principle a reality in your life.

How to change the quality of your life in an instant.

Here's an example of how the power of refocusing works. Have you ever thought someone did something wrong to you? You got angry and hurt but when you talked to the person about the issue, you found out that they had no bad intentions at all. What happened to your hurt and anger? It went away instantly because you were no longer focused on it—you got a new perspective.

We can train ourselves to get a new perspective on everything that happens to us. Another example: There was a time in my life that whenever something bad happened to me I blamed it on God. I got so angry. Then one day I realized that it was not God's nature to cause bad things to happen. My view of God changed instantly because I changed my focus. Then I realized that stuff happens in life – but I don't have to let it crush me.

You can actually stop in the midst of a bad day and change the way you view it. Instantly your attitude and emotions can positively change.

One more example: As I drove to work I was thinking of the busy day ahead of me. When I arrived I realized that I had forgotten my parking garage key-card. I was already running late and was having a bad day. I had to drive back home and get it, adding an hour to my already long Los Angeles commute.

I decided to apply this principle and I changed my focus instantly by saying, "Thank you God for giving me extra time in the car to pray and listen to a tape." I turned a bad day into a good one. By the time I arrived back at the office I had more peace than normal and people noticed. Learning to change your focus is a step towards renewing your mind.

"Do not conform any longer to the pattern of this world, but be transformed by the renewing of your mind. Then you will be able to test and approve what God's will is—his good, pleasing and perfect will." (Romans 12:2)

"Finally, brothers, whatever is true, whatever is noble, whatever is right, whatever is pure, whatever is lovely, whatever is admirable—if anything is excellent or praiseworthy—think about such things." (Philippians 4:8)

Decide ahead of time where to put your focus (this is your emotional energy). It will take intentional effort on your part but you can learn to turn bad situations into good ones. You can learn to make the most of every situation. Where your focus goes, your energy flows. It is not worth getting upset! As you learn to redirect your focus it will free you up to begin to plan how you want things to be instead. This is how your creative flow (connection to God) gets reestablished and solutions to various issues in your life will come more easily to you.

Doug Addison

Remedy 4: Realize that God Wants to Use Your Current Situation

There are so many of us who have prophetic promises from God about operating at a higher level of ministry but are currently in a job or situation that we have little passion for. Perhaps you need a financial breakthrough that will allow you to freely do all the things that God is calling you to. God spoke to me that a key for this breakthrough may lie in your current situation.

My breakthrough

In 1988, God began speaking to me about being in full time ministry. A few years later I got serious about pursuing ministry training, but the problem was that I still needed to work my full time job to make a living. So I started doing self-study courses and volunteered what little free time I had at ministries that were doing what I felt called to. It seemed that I would never have the opportunity to serve God with the freedom I wanted and have the money to get the training I needed. Then God showed me that I needed to stop living my life thinking about how it will be in the future, begin enjoying the present, and be grateful each day for the job I had at the time.

"Whatever you do, work at it with all your heart, as working for the Lord, not for men, since you know that you will receive an inheritance from the Lord as a reward. It is the Lord Christ you are serving." (Colossians 3:23–24)

In 1993 everything changed when I started working at my job as if I were working for God. I was working in San Francisco at the time, and my boss and most of my fellow employees were not Christian. In fact, most people were very hostile towards Christians in the workplace. In spite of that I decided to use my God-given spiritual gifts to help people at work instead of complaining to God about my feelings of being stuck. I started praying and interceding for the company I worked for, and we started seeing dramatic results. I would get words of knowledge and share them as "ideas I got while praying," and the owner began to attribute my prayers with the company's success.

As a result, I received bonuses and a couple of years later, when I approached them about transitioning from my corporate job into ministry, they were helpful by keeping me on part time. Eventually they hired me back as a contractor for five times the pay! This extraordinary favor allowed me to transition into full time ministry and provided funding to plant our first church. God opened the doors, but it was a result of me changing my attitude towards my situation. God used my current job and a group of non-Christians to bless me. Years later God used the experiences I had at that job to help develop my message of Prophetic Evangelism that is now being taught all over the world.

Change your situation

God wants to use your current situation to bless you and release finances and favor into your life. The key is learning to be content and working at whatever it is you are doing as if you are working for God Himself. This does not only pertain to jobs, but also to being in school, relationships or whatever situation you are in.

The Bible tells us that we can do incredible things through God's strength. Since God's love and power is limitless, what we can accomplish through His Holy Spirit has no limits as well. If we are unhappy and anxious about our situation, it can create limits to what we can do through God. Allowing God's love to flow through us, being content, and having gratitude can change the spiritual atmosphere around us and ultimately create an environment in which blessings are drawn to us.

"I know what it is to be in need, and I know what it is to have plenty. I have learned the secret of being content in any and every situation, whether well fed or hungry, whether living in plenty or in want. I can do everything through him who gives me strength." (Philippians 4:12–13)

If you feel frustrated or stuck, begin to find good things in your life right now. Here are a few tips on how to change your current situation. Give thanks to God for all that He has done for you. Make a list of blessings and things you are grateful for. Think about the positive things you like about people in your life. If you are married, what are the things that originally drew you to your spouse? Learn to recognize and help draw attention to the good things in other people. Ask yourself, who can you encourage or help today? Who can you help practically?

"God can do anything, you know—far more than you could ever imagine or guess or request in your wildest dreams! He does it not

by pushing us around but by working within us, his Spirit deeply and gently within us." (Ephesians 3:20, The Message)

Remedy 5: Develop the Lost Art of Revelation

We can begin experiencing a radical turn around in our spiritual lives and overcome Spiritual Identity Theft when we simply go back to the basics of the things we believe, and find ways to make them a daily lifestyle. Several years ago, while living in Los Angeles, I discovered that my day would flow much better if I spent 30–45 minutes a day doing a focused prayer walk and 15 minutes or so reading and meditating on the Bible. The results were so amazing that I was able to reduce my daily work hours because I knew what I needed to focus on at any given time.

When we moved to North Carolina, a rural area with snakes, bugs, humidity and four seasons, I tried so hard to keep my "Hour of God's Power" going, but I was not able to be consistent. Eventually I sank back into the tyranny of the urgent and lost the edge I once had. It was pretty ironic that I was living in Moravian Falls, under an open Heaven environment in a cabin that was spiritually active with angelic activity, and I had trouble praying at the level I needed to in order to stay at a deep intimate level with God. It is out of relationship and intimacy with God that everything will flow. Don't get me wrong, I still prayed and studied, but not at my fullest potential. Part of this may have been that, for me, California and the west coast is the land of my anointing. For some reason I fit best in the land of "fruits, flakes, and nuts!"

After moving back to California, I noticed that I began having more spiritual experiences with God and found it easy to get back into an Hour of God's Power. I saw the changes and benefits almost immediately. While on my prayer walk, reading the Bible and taking a shower (in that order), I started to gain deep revelation about my day-to-day situations just like I had discovered several years ago while keeping this practice. It is amazing that you know this in your head, but getting yourself to do it makes all the difference. I began making Matthew 6:33 my guiding verse:

"But seek first his kingdom and his righteousness, and all these things will be given to you as well." (Matthew 6:33)

The secret to spiritual growth

We can know the truth of the Bible, but if we are not actually doing it, then we are lacking a tangible revelation of the truth. Once we get a revelation of any verse or principle, it becomes alive in us and gives us a spiritual push forward. If we take the revelation a step farther, and we do something to practically use it or apply it in our life, then we begin to advance. If we do it regularly and make a habit or lifestyle from it, then momentum kicks in and we go to an entirely new level that few people are aware exists. If you take it even further and show others how to do it, you move ahead even more in your maturity, and you gain more wisdom and anointing because the more you give, the more you will receive. It really has been the secret to my success in my relationship with God and my ministry.

Some people misunderstand these Kingdom principles and push forward, making them rules instead of relational opportunities to be a conduit for God. The difference between striving and actively pursuing is that those who strive do not have the revelation and are doing it out of motivations like: "I am supposed to;" "It is good for me but I really don't like it;" "I might get something out of it;" or "It makes me a better Christian," etc. When something becomes a rule, you lose intimacy with the giver of the gifts, and you begin to lack grace and love for yourself and others.

The lost art of revelation

The principle of revelation is alive when God makes Himself real to us (Revelation 19:10). Those who commit their lives to Christ through a revelation of God usually experience a much more fulfilling spiritual life from those who do it out of a decision based on guilt, logic, or rules. Sometimes altar calls motivate people to come forward for the wrong reasons. When the Spirit draws us, as opposed to guilt or condemnation, then we connect with God at a much deeper level that is based on love, and we will see a greater level of change in our lives.

I have had several very deep revelations of verses from the Bible that have changed my life and now the lives of many. Most of my messages came through revelation which occurred during my Hour of God's Power. You can go through my material or that of others and pick up principles that will change your life to some degree. But if you will allow these principles to enlighten and motivate you through the Holy Spirit, then you cannot help but impact the world for God.

The Hour of God's Power does not have to be an hour. It can be whatever you are comfortable with and feel God directing you to do. There are times for me when it is more and other times when it is less. The key is to grasp the revelation that things like reading the Bible, praying, worshipping, art, and yes, even exercising help you connect with God because you are a temple of the Holy Spirit. When you connect with God through intimacy and relationship, then you will want to spend more time with Him instead of doing it because you have to.

"I keep asking that the God of our Lord Jesus Christ, the glorious Father, may give you the Spirit of wisdom and revelation, so that you may know him better. I pray also that the eyes of your heart may be enlightened in order that you may know the hope to which he has called you, the riches of his glorious inheritance in the saints, and his incomparably great power for us who believe. That power is like the working of his mighty strength ..." (Ephesians 1:17–19)

Ask God to give you eyes to see, ears that hear, and a spirit that perceives what it is He is calling you to right now!

Remedy 6: Find Your Destiny

I have been talking about destiny and life purpose and the fact that Satan wants to steal your spiritual identity to keep you from advancing and maturing. There are so many people today who are searching for the purpose for which they were created. A desire for purpose is rooted in our human nature. Too often, many of us try to fill this with things like careers, status, cars, or the perfect relationship or family. None of these are bad in and of themselves. However, they will not bring true fulfillment in life. Our purpose and destiny can ultimately only be filled through the good news of God's love.

There is a good chance you have heard me talk or write about this before. That is because I have been saying it over and over since I discovered it in 1994. It is the entire message of Jesus summed up in three verses and it relates to you discovering more about your purpose and destiny.

Jesus summed up the entire good news message when in Matthew 4:19, He said, "Come, follow me ..." Following Jesus in all that we do is the first place to start in finding your destiny.

In Matthew 22:37–39, *"Jesus replied: 'Love the Lord your God with all your heart and with all your soul and with all your mind.' This is the first and greatest commandment. And the second is like it: 'Love your neighbor as yourself.'"* We must love God, love other people, and love ourselves.

Finally, in Matthew 28:19–20, Jesus said, " ... *go and make disciples of all nations, baptizing them in the name of the Father and of the Son and of the Holy Spirit, and teaching them to obey everything I have commanded you ... * " In other words, help other people and in so doing we end up making the world a better place.

Your destiny is a unique assignment from God that starts with learning to follow Jesus, loving God and others, and helping others to do the same. You cannot go wrong if you build your life on this foundation. I like to think of finding your life purpose or destiny as being similar to a "connect the dots" drawing. At any given time your goal is to go to the next dot. Too often we want to rush ahead and we miss all the necessary growing opportunities that God has for us. Destiny reveals itself over time and the more we pursue it, the clearer it becomes.

In order to find your destiny it helps to understand that we all have been uniquely created by God and we all have a purpose. The Apostle Paul refers to Christians as a body made up of separate parts (1 Corinthians 12:12–13). We need to find our unique function and fit in life. Our purpose is intended to be fulfilled in who we are in God. We must allow God to renew our minds and our lives through His Spirit in order to fulfill our purpose among other Christians. Being in relationship and community with others is essential to our growth.

When I first became a Christian I felt strongly that my destiny involved being in full-time ministry. The problem with this is that only two percent of all Christians can actually fill paid ministry positions. I realized later, that in God's eyes, we are all ministers and we are all in full-time ministry! I tried quitting my corporate job and working at my church. I found out quickly that though it was a good cause, it was not my unique ability to do so. I went from there and started a computer networking business in San Francisco that got me back into contact with people who needed to be encouraged with God's love and acceptance.

What we do and how we act on a daily basis is what builds the foundation that will take us to our ultimate purpose in life. It will help to realize that your destiny is shaped by what you do in your day-to-day life. Remember the movie Karate Kid? Mr. Miagi taught Daniel to be a master in martial arts by first having him wax his car, paint his fence, and move a bunch of rocks. The skills he needed later were practiced in practical everyday jobs. Your destiny is the same.

God has been leaving you clues about your destiny all your life. I don't have time to go into all the details in this short book. I have written other resources that have practical exercises to walk you through the process of finding and fulfilling your destiny. At the end of this book I list some additional resources that will help you.

Here are a few essential destiny builders that we can all practice on a daily basis.

Recognize and eliminate unhealthy habits. This may be a lifelong process but we all need to be motivated by God's Spirit and not our own desires. I had some bad habits of avoiding things I did not want to do. I also would overeat when I got stressed out. I found ways to work through these patterns and now they no longer dominate my life.

Develop good new habits. We can refocus our lives and renew ourselves by spending regular time reading the Bible and praying. We all know this but doing it takes effort. God wants to give us the desires of our heart (Psalm 37:4). That happens after our heart is in line with His. Each day that I get up, no matter how busy I am I remind myself of the fact that I have to *"Seek first the Kingdom of God ..."* (Matthew 6:33). I also have developed new habits of exercise, eating better, and staying up on my relationships with other people.

Be generous. Be a giver. This is not just about money, although giving money shows where your heart is. Give your time, energy, affection, focus and attention to all that you do. If you need something in your life like wisdom, revelation, love, or money then you may want to try giving to others in the areas you need. This is like spiritually "back flushing" your pool filter so to speak. It removes clogs and allows the Spirit to flow through us again.

Be grateful. A grateful spirit will attract blessing. Whatever you sow you will reap. If we are not grateful then we will not recognize a blessing when it comes. Most people grumble and complain and they wonder why their life is full of negativity and bad circumstances. You can turn your life around today by dropping out of the grumblers club. Being grateful is a spiritual principle that allows good things to flow back to you. I used to complain about the bad service I got on airlines. I was always stuck in the back of the plane with a bad seat, a bad meal and people being irritated at me. I turned this around by being grateful and putting in compliments everywhere I went. Now I get free first class upgrades all the time. I get better customer service too.

Learn to love. How we treat other people reflects our character. Godly character is required for all of us. How we love other people is most likely how we love God. Remember that love covers over a multitude of sins, love conquers all, and love never fails! You can check yourself on this and see if you are loving people. It starts with how you act behind the wheel of your car. For some reason we forget that the other car contains a real person. Don't let other people who are having a bad day drag you into their swirl. Get to a place where you love others, pray for them and encourage them. You will have a lot more peace in your life.

Develop a "breakthrough lifestyle." Most people live a lifestyle of avoidance. Instead, find things that you are putting off and do them. Even a small simple task, done daily or weekly towards what you feel called to do, may not look like much when we do them but they build over time. A small degree of change or accomplishment done consistently will result in massive results after six weeks. Imagine all that growth stacking up after six months or even a year and it can be done with a minimal amount of effort. I do this at the beginning of every week. It is amazing how much you can accomplish with very little effort if you are consistent.

Finding and fulfilling your destiny is not as hard as one might think. Build your life on a firm foundation that will allow you to accomplish all that God has in mind for you. Believe that you can do it! Look for things that ignite passion within you. Take small steps consistently. Find someone who is doing what you want to do and study what they have learned. Do something today like read a book, do internet research, make a phone call, sign up for a class, or get some practical training. It is never too late.

"I can do everything through him who gives me strength." (Philippians 4:13)

Remedy 7: God's Good Intentions for You

We all need to make some types of changes in our lives. Positive change happens when you make a decision to do something and take steps to make it reality. Start small, stay consistent, and over time momentum will build. Transformation occurs when you go beyond your own strength of decision-making, tap into God's ultimate power and wisdom to renew your thinking and your behavior, and combine this with practicing the art of good choices.

You can change your life, but transformation occurs when you practice things enough that they become automatic. Transformation requires both God's power and your good choices. Most people either try to do it in their own strength and leave God out, or they focus entirely on being spiritual but fail to be proactive. A balance of both is required.

A really great thing about God is that He sees us as who we are becoming through His love and power. As He looks at your life, He knows your past, understands your present, and can see your future, all at the same time. His love, mercy, and grace are unfathomable. Imagine the possibilities if we could see ourselves the same way that God sees us. Much of the time we are not able to see our purpose and destiny with much clarity, so we are required to rely on faith.

The principle of faith allows us to trust that there is something special and unique for us, even if our experiences have been the opposite. Sometimes there is great resistance or even setbacks before we are able to get into the fullness of God's desires for us.

"Now faith is being sure of what we hope for and certain of what we do not see." (Hebrews 11:1)

We need to be certain of the fact that God has nothing but good intentions for us, even though we may not see them yet. You'll see this in the powerful biblical principle:

"For I know the plans I have for you," declares the Lord, "plans to prosper you and not to harm you, plans to give you hope and a future." (Jeremiah 29:11)

These are God's intentions for us. His plans are to prosper us, to give us hope and a future. If you read on, you'll see the benefits of grasping this.

"Then [after you discover God's plans for you] you will call upon me and come and pray to me, and I will listen to you. You will seek me and find me when you seek me with all your heart." (Jeremiah 29:12-13)

We must see what God is doing in our lives and work with Him to bring it about. It's time to take a stand against what Satan has in mind for us and come into line with God's wonderful intentions for us.

God's true destiny is found in Jeremiah 29:11–12. He wants us to prosper, live a life of no harm (or fear), give us a hope and a future and answered prayer. How good is that! I have found that many people have the opposite in their lives. Instead of prosperity they have a poverty mindset and debt. Instead of living a life of confidence of no harm coming to them, they are living in fear. Instead of having hope they are hopeless, distressed, and even depressed. Instead of living a life with a clear vision, they have no clue about their destiny. And instead of seeing their prayers answered consistently, they often give up praying because they are discouraged.

These are all symptoms of Spiritual Identity Theft. If you have any of these negative things in your life you can turn them around today by asking God to remove the negative and bring His positive promises into your life.

Let's do that right now by praying this prayer:

"Father in Heaven, we ask that you remove any poverty or debt from our lives and replace it with prosperity and blessings. Release to us new strategies on how we can make more money and spend less. God, we ask that you would remove any fear or mindsets that we might have that are keeping us from moving forward with boldness. And we command that all hopelessness and despair leave our minds and be replaced with sound and clear thinking. God show us our destinies and reveal our futures. Remove any plans and strategies of Satan to steal our identities in you. In Jesus name, amen."

Begin to watch for ways that God answers this prayer that you just prayed. It is a good idea to keep a journal or write down when things start happening. Most of the time we forget to look back and see how far we have come. Or when God reveals a new strategy to you, be sure to write it down so you don't forget.

It is good to make a habit of listing out things that God speaks to you. If He gives you a strategy then take some steps towards it. Oftentimes we don't know what to do next but there are other times when God is revealing it to us and we are not attentive to what He has said.

"If people can't see what God is doing, they stumble all over themselves; but when they attend to what he reveals, they are most blessed." (Proverbs 29:18, The Message)

As you go through the process of discovering the Spiritual Identity Theft in your life, you'll find that it is similar to the story of David in 1 Samuel 30. David had a prophetic promise to be king of Israel and was anointed by Samuel, but his timing had not yet come. King Saul had been trying to kill David and then the enemy came and stole their possessions, families and burned their city to the ground. David was greatly distressed but he encouraged himself in the Lord. They recovered everything and things changed at that point and David went from running away to a new place of ruling and authority.

Just because God declared that David would be King, did not make it happen automatically. David had to get up and go fight for it against all odds. Many people today do not understand this and are sitting back waiting for God to do it for them. It is time to encourage ourselves in the Lord and not pull back. It is time to no longer believe the lies of the enemy but to grab hold of our only reality, which is God's Word and will for our lives. It is time to pursue! This is truly an exciting time to be alive. Don't give up!

I want to give you a prayer strategy that worked wonders in my life. I saw an immediate turn around in our ministry and personal life by praying the following daily for a few weeks:

- God, reveal what promises are for now and what are for later (timing)
- Show us what the enemy does not want us to see (discernment)
- God, allow us to be seen as You see us, not as the enemy wants us to be seen (favor)
- Repay and release what was stolen and held back by the enemy (justice)
- Show us how to practically respond (wisdom)

Your Identity is in Christ

The foundation of my life is this: in Christ, I am a new creation, and all the old thoughts and behaviors no longer have power over me. I am being renewed every day with God's love and character. I share in God's divine nature because God's Spirit lives in me.

I am free from condemnation and have the strength to live my life free of despairing thoughts and the competing desires of my flesh. I am God's workmanship, created to do good works, which God has prepared ahead of time for me to accomplish. I am more than a conqueror through God who loves me. I have a clear mind and can make good decisions. I am increasing daily in faith, strength, wisdom, and love. I am able to love others because God has first loved me.

May God richly bless you on your journey and I want to encourage you to share what you have learned with someone else.

Other Resources from Doug Addison

Personal Development God's Way
272 pages
People everywhere want to know their life purpose and destiny. God's desire for us all is nothing but the best. Personal Development God's Way was developed after Doug Addison spent a lifetime of studying why some Christian's lives change radically and others do not. This book is full of practical

Accelerating Into Your Life's Purpose
10 Audio CDs & 62 page Journal
Discover your destiny, awaken passion, and transform your life with this 10 day interactive program. Designed to reveal your life's desires, remove obstacles, and create a written plan for what to focus on next.

Kingdom Financial Strategies
2 CD Audio Set & Study Guide
Doug Addison uncovers many financial principles of which most people are unaware. As you apply these principles to your life you will begin to experience lasting change in the area of money, ministry, and business.

For more information visit

www.dougaddison.com or call (800) 507-7853